From Key Stage 2 to Key Stage 3: Smoothing the Transfer for Pupils with Learning Difficulties

Contents

Acknowledgements

The author wishes to thank the following Suffolk teachers who responded to her circular letter and who gave her invaluable information about pupils who transfer to their secondary schools: Sue Corp, Lesley Garnett, Sue Healey, Val James, Penny Knights, Pauline Mursell-Head, Viv Salisbury, Pat Stiven. Thanks also go to Jean Salt for a description of the transition arrangements in her comprehensive school; to those who read the manuscript and gave constructive and helpful comments, especially to Kerry Ekins and Tricia Craven; and to others who responded to the request for ideas.

Introduction

This book discusses the problems pupils with learning difficulties might experience when transferring from mainstream primary to mainstream secondary schools. Learning difficulties in the context of this book cover specific learning difficulties (dyslexia et al) and general to moderate learning difficulties where pupils' all-round cognitive abilities are weak. Emotional/behavioural issues are also considered.

Although this book does not cover problems concerning special schooling; although it does not deal with issues of sensory or physical impairment; although specialised issues such as autism or Asperger's Syndrome are not discussed in any depth, the issues presented are common to all pupils who move from Key Stage 2 to Key Stage 3 when this move takes place from one establishment to another. Often LEA Support Services offer expert help with pupils with very particular special needs. Thus, although pupils requiring additional resources and support because of particular disabilities and learning needs will have particular transfer outcomes, issues deliberated within this book will still apply in general terms.

Some pupils change schools within their secondary years because of parental preference or because of a house move. They are required to enter a school where friendship groups are firmly established, where the school structure may be unlike their previous one and where even lessons may be different. There are suggestions within the book which will help to make these pupils feel less awkward and more at ease on transfer.

The book aims to offer suggestions to teachers in both sectors so that they can make transfer easier and more comfortable for themselves, their colleagues, their pupils and the pupils' parents/carers. It also gives some hints for how parents/carers can help and be helped. There may be issues for parents when they request a particular secondary school but are allocated an alternative. If this becomes a question of dispute between the home, school and LEA then there can be added problems for the pupil. There may also be issues of inclusion which will have to be resolved within the particular LEA or within the particular school.

It is recognised that not all LEAs solely have primary and secondary schooling. Some LEAs are organised on a three phase model with first schools, middle schools and upper schools. In such an organisational framework the middle school often acts as a bridge between the one teacher–one class model of the first (primary) school and the many teachers to one class model of the upper (secondary) school. However, the majority of mainstream pupils move from primary to secondary schools at the end of their Year 6 in Key Stage 2. This book contains information which can be used for other transfer situations.

The problems of transferring from one school to another have been recognised by the DfEE and in January 1999 a review was commissioned to look into this (as well as transition within schools from one year group to another). Although this was not specifically about pupils with special educational needs there were indications that two out of every five pupils failed to make the expected progress during the year after their transfer. Extra resources have been allocated to schools in 13 LEAs to run pilot schemes to investigate what can be set up to help problems at transfer. These will stress the importance of teaching literacy and numeracy across the curriculum; encouraging the teaching of thinking skills and investigating how pupils themselves can evaluate problems and areas to work on. The results of these projects should be of particular interest to all schools.

The differences between the primary and the secondary sector

Primary schools

It might be suppositional to generalise but most primary schools have at least seven classes, one for each year group excluding the Nursery sector. Of course there are small village schools, some with just two classes, and some very large primary schools which are larger than the smaller secondary schools. However, the majority of Year 6 pupils move to secondary schools which are larger than the ones in which they have spent their primary years.

Except in the largest of the primary schools pupils are well able to get to know all the staff members and for the teachers to get to know them. They are usually well aware of the 'new' teacher to whom they will transfer after a year and they stay with their class peers for most of their lessons. Thus they build up a stable group of peers, friends, acquaintances and rivals. Since the introduction of *The National Literacy Strategy* and *The National Numeracy Strategy* schools have been experimenting with class and group organisation. In some larger primary schools parallel–aged classes have been split and often two classes have been divided into three so that a 'bottom set' can be created. In this way those pupils with literacy and numeracy problems are set within smaller groups. Some LEAs retain Learning Support Services who employ support teachers who sometimes offer withdrawal teaching sessions for literacy and sometimes for numeracy. Similar teachers are sometimes employed by the schools. Occasionally some year groups come together for subjects such as games or at times teachers with a 'specialism' are able to teach classes other than their register class. Non-teaching headteachers and deputy headteachers also take some classes for some areas of the curriculum. Nevertheless, it can be stated that children in the primary sector are taught in an arrangement which, to them, appears organised, stable and secure.

Secondary schools

Secondary education is quite different. Because a number of primary schools feed into the local secondary school, pupils are required to make acquaintance with the pupils from these other schools. They might be separated from their original peers. The secondary schools are large with specialist teachers. There is seldom any class teaching from form tutors except for PSHE so pupils have to relate to many teachers throughout the week. They have to remember their names, their faces and their personalities. No longer are they in one classroom area with a base in which they feel secure, where they have a desk or some kind of storage container for their books and belongings. In the secondary school they might have a locker in a cloakroom or corridor area but generally they carry their daily or even weekly belongings with them from room to room. Although they have a form tutor it is quite difficult to make a close relationship with this teacher. There are so many staff members to get to know and so many classrooms and specialist rooms to find. For some pupils this change of situation can become traumatic and fearful.

Transfer in general terms

Therefore, transferring from the primary to the secondary school can be a difficult and even an apprehensive time for many pupils. For those with learning difficulties it can be quite troublesome and worrying unless there has been good preparation to alleviate transfer difficulties. Secondary schools set up excellent open days and primary liaison days. These will differ in different LEAs and even within the same LEA and the quality of such occasions and their organisation may be very different but most schools arrange open days for parents where the secondary school 'sells' itself to the public. In these days of parental choice schools are keen to 'persuade' and encourage parents to send their children to them.

Once the intake is organised, especially in those LEAs where it is customary for primary school pupils to transfer to their neighbourhood secondary schools, there is usually a day in the summer term for Year 6 pupils to visit and get a feel for their new school. In some schools older pupils take charge of the younger newcomers and take them on a conducted visit of the school. The Year 6 pupils meet the staff and sometimes join lessons, especially those which they might not have experienced in the primary sector.

One secondary school organises the following:

- An art afternoon where present pupils work with prospective pupils
- A science afternoon with science lessons all afternoon
- An induction day where pupils meet their form and have a day of lessons with the teachers they will have as a group when they come to the secondary school

- Year 6 pupils are invited to concert rehearsals, play rehearsals
- Tours of the buildings are given on evening visits
- Evening introductions to canteen food and dinner hall routines
- An evening visit where the timetable is explained to both parents and pupils
- Form captains (Year 10 pupils) meet Year 7 classes prior to them starting at the secondary school and they explain their role in looking after pupils

---

Another secondary school organises the following to counteract any anxiety that is felt that particular primary pupils might have about transfer:

- The primary pupil is invited to come and spend a day with a Year 7 class (and occasionally this will be a class where another pupil is known so a link can be set up)
- The day is chosen so that the timetable includes some subjects which the pupil enjoys
- Where possible there would be the opportunity for the pupil to join a withdrawal group in Maths or English within the Learning Support Faculty (but this is not a priority)
- The visit is confirmed with a letter of invitation detailing the day's timetable and giving lunch and equipment requirements
- The form tutor, the subject teachers involved in the day and the Learning Support Assistants (LSAs) working within the classes are primed
- The Year 7 pupil and the primary guest are invited to visit the Learning Support games room at lunchtime
- After the visit the subject teachers feed back any information and comments to the Special Educational Needs Co-ordinator (SENCO).

This scheme has run for about 10 years and has proved very successful in helping allay anxieties about transfer to the secondary school.

Heads of year and other pastoral staff visit the primary schools and see the pupils in their familiar settings. Information on pupils is exchanged and often the secondary school SENCO will also visit to discuss any special educational needs issues. Some secondary schools even set up a special needs visit where the identified primary pupils on the special needs register or with a Statement of Special Educational Needs are given a second visit.

However well organised pre-transfer arrangements have been, the first day at secondary school is as difficult for some pupils as was their first day at primary school. But this time their parents cannot stay with them and they cannot cry or show signs of anxiety. They have to 'grin and bear it'. They are expected to be 'grown up'. For some pupils with learning difficulties the first weeks in the secondary school must be a terrible and quite fearful experience. Many of these pupils might not know how to express their uncertainties, their worries and their problems. How they continue with their school-lives, how they cope with their new experiences and how teachers cope with them, depend on these first weeks.

Pupils with learning difficulties and the problems they experience

There are two types of learning difficulties and two sets of issues which will be covered within this book.

General learning difficulties

Pupils may have general all-round learning difficulties and sometimes these can be given the label 'moderate'. Their pace of learning is slow. They have below average cognitive abilities. Their attainments in the basic skills are weak as they find learning to read, spell, understand, cope with written work and mathematics very difficult. On standardised tests and in the Key Stage 2 SATs they score at a level of a much younger pupil. Their general level of attainment will be significantly below that of their peers and below their own age level. Many will have speech and language difficulties and some may also have poor social skills. There is also the possibility that they might show signs of emotional and behavioural difficulties. These children find all areas of the curriculum difficult as well as finding the transfer from being a primary pupil to a secondary pupil a hazardous experience.

Specific learning difficulties (e.g. dyslexia)

These pupils have particular and sometimes quite significant difficulties in reading, spelling, written work and coping with mathematics which is not typical of their level of performance in other areas of the curriculum. They often have cognitive abilities in the average to above average range and have good oral abilities and knowledge of words. In areas of the curriculum which do not require much literacy or numeracy, they may cope well. Like their counterparts with general learning difficulties, pupils with specific learning difficulties score at a low attainment level on tests but, of course, these are not necessarily indicative of their general level of ability. Many of these pupils become extremely frustrated by their problems and will show signs of low self-esteem which are displayed in emotional and behavioural problems. Transfer to the secondary school can be just as difficult for these pupils, especially when they have to expose their problems to newcomers, to unknown teachers and to peers from other primary schools.

Emotional and behavioural difficulties

As has been mentioned, both the above groups of children may exhibit emotional and behavioural problems. These can be linked with frustration because the work might appear too difficult and not adequately differentiated or with lack of self-esteem where they view themselves as failures. If their method of expressing their anger, frustration and lack of self-confidence results in unacceptable in-school behaviours then their first weeks in the secondary sector get off to a poor start. Even if these behaviours are low-level disruptions such as becoming the class clown, making irritating noises, calling out or being frequently off-task rather than being major problems, such as defiantly and rudely confronting the member of staff, teachers will deal with the inappropriate behaviours quite severely. Teachers need to set the standard of discipline for their classes and find it hard to cope with exploring the reasons why the occasional pupil does not conform.

Pupils who are withdrawn because of their emotional problems are less easy to spot because of their coping strategies within classes. These pupils are 'keeping their heads down' and trying to make sure that they are not asked questions or expected to contribute to any activity, especially if this requires literacy skills. In a large secondary school where some teachers teach many classes, these quiet and apparently unassuming pupils sometimes go unrecognised for a considerable length of time, making it hard for the staff member to recall their face when discussing their progress at parents' evenings.

Issues of low self-esteem
Self-esteem needs a reference point which is usually outside the pupil where he or she matches him or herself against the prowess of others. Often pupils with specific learning difficulties who cannot come to terms with their own problems perceive themselves to be unintelligent and failures whereas their ideal self wishes to be successful and competent. These pupils often become locked into a circular system of anxiety where their problems with literacy acquisition prevent them from trying because then they might make mistakes. Mistakes will make them seem unintelligent and this fuels the anxiety. Even if such pupils have coped within the primary sector, their confidence can dip considerably once confronted by the 'unknown' in the secondary school.

Because of issues concerning exclusion from school, LEAs are examining ways of helping younger pupils within the primary sector to cope with their anger, frustration and anxieties.

One LEA has set up a short-term project where an LSA has been appointed to work within one town pyramid which comprises a large comprehensive school and five primary schools. She asked teachers within the latter to identify pupils for whom there was concern in terms of their behavioural and self-esteem problems. They should either have IEPs (individual education plans) which targeted behaviour or who were felt to be socially isolated or bullied. Fifteen pupils were chosen and most had learning problems but a few were seemingly intelligent but over-emotional and apparently unable to cope with their peers. These pupils would be allocated individual support sessions where the LSA would get to know them, help them complete work and target their low self-esteem and behavioural problems. After a while the individual sessions would become group-based. For two terms the LSA would work intensively with these identified pupils and in the autumn term she would transfer with them into their feeder comprehensive school. Support would continue. It is hoped that she will help raise their self-esteems, will enable them to take responsibility for their behaviours and that they will settle well into the larger school community. Parents will be contacted to see if they see any difference in their child. This is a project where everyone is learning as time goes on. If it is seen to work then maybe schools will be able to use ideas etc. to help their own pupils within their own settings using their own staff members.

Problems on transfer

This section will list and cluster the various problems pupils with learning difficulties might encounter once they transfer to the secondary sector. These problems have been gathered from teachers and pupils within secondary schools and can be subdivided into those concerned with organisation, with learning issues, with relationships and with adult expectations.

Organisational problems
These can be divided into two sections. The first depends on skills of spatial awareness, visual memory and independence. They are:

- using the school bus or public transport
- size of the school site
- the organisation of the school
- finding their way about, the geography of the school
- moving from room to room.

The second involves personal organisation on a smaller scale where the pupils have to learn how to cope within classes and at break and lunchtimes. These are:

- having to move after a particular period of time (50+ minutes) and having to get out equipment, then pack it up and move on
- managing own property
- carrying everything around (e.g. PE kit, DT equipment in addition to text books, current folder and general equipment)
- providing the correct equipment for particular lessons
- always having to write with a pen
- reading and following the weekly or fortnightly timetable
- planning homework and using a homework diary, recording homework accurately
- what to do and where to go at playtime
- coping with late lunchtimes and their own hunger
- using the canteen, food prices, queuing, knowing where to sit
- managing own money.

Learning problems
- the range of new vocabulary used by subject staff
- reading core subject area words

- size of handwriting (especially where planners and diaries are concerned)
- note making and making sense of these at a later time
- copying from the board or OHP
- taking notes from oral dictation
- recording homework
- coping with homework
- working in class in different ways as expected by various teachers
- coping with subjects not yet experienced
- development of listening skills
- using the library
- using CD-ROMs and the Internet.

Self-esteem and relationship problems
- relating to many different members of staff
- worrying about coping with so many teachers
- knowing where to go if there is a problem (which teacher or adult to see)
- having a new LSA
- going from being the oldest in the school to being the youngest
- tales told to them by older siblings and older pupils of 'things' that are done to Year 7 pupils
- issues of bullying
- making new friends.

Adult expectations
- parental expectations of their child's ability to cope
- parental concerns that their child will be unable to cope
- the secondary school's expectations of the pupil based on reported ability
- the secondary school's expectations of the pupil based on its experience and knowledge of older siblings.

Pupils' perceived problems
Mentioned above are the tales that are told to frighten the younger pupil. Often primary school pupils become very nervous about 'what might happen if..., what could I do when..., how would I cope with...?' One SENCO wrote that a 'Top Ten Catastrophe' list could be collated in the primary school. Everyone would then discuss what could be done, whether these were real or made-up. If they could be dealt with light-heartedly, there would be the chance that the more nervous pupil would stop brooding and be able to deal with any problems that might arise.

Top Ten Catastrophes
1. You've heard about bog washing! Will it happen to you?
2. You've heard about being thrown into the prickle bush. Will it happen to you?
3. You've forgotten your PE kit. What might you do?
4. You haven't done your French homework. What might you do?
5. Your coat is missing from the classroom. Who might you go to?
6. You don't understand the Maths work. What might you do?
7. Your planner has jam on it. How can you explain this?
8. Your young sister has torn your History book. How can you explain this?
9. A Year 10 pupil has taken your dinner money. Who might you go to?
10. You are given a detention? What happens?

How the primary school
can help with the problems

Like the previous section the problems will be subdivided. Not all of them can be worked on in the primary sector but there are many issues which can be either simulated in school or experienced at first hand. Ideally the primary school should start the 'secondary experience' programme from the beginning of Year 6 rather than waiting until the summer term. If it can be built into the PSHE programme with parents becoming aware and involved then the pupils should be able to take the information within their stride. Many of them will not know which secondary schools they will be transferring to but several of the problem areas are general. It will be easier for those primary schools which transfer all or the majority of their pupils to the same secondary school to deal with the actual school than those primary schools which send pupils to many schools. There may be organisational issues for some primary schools which will need careful planning.

One primary school encourages all Year 6 pupils to help in Community Projects. The SENCO keeps a record so that each pupil has:

- spoken publicly
- explained the working of the classes or displays to other children in school and to adults visiting the school
- acted as mentors, play companions and general helpers to children in the early years classes.

In this way the pupils are helped to become more independent and confident.

Organisational problems
Finding the way around the school
The size and complexity of the secondary school can cause much concern where primary school pupils are concerned. Even in larger primary schools there are those pupils who may find it hard to take messages to different areas of the school such as the staff room. From an

early age primary pupils should be encouraged to find their own way around their school, at first with a friend and later independently. Pupils who seem to have particular problems, either with memory or because of shyness, should be given tasks such as taking visitors around the school.

> Steven, like a great many Year 6 pupils, answered in the following way when asked if he was looking forward to going to the secondary school. 'In a way I am but I am afraid of getting lost.'

Using maps
Although it is not possible to help the pupil to become aware of the layout of the secondary school until a place has been allotted, there can be general work given on maps and layout.

Later when the actual school is known (or possible schools known) the secondary school staff and the primary school staff can liaise and this might even necessitate the latter visiting the secondary schools to gain some idea of the schools' layouts. Year 6 classes can be given photocopies of the layouts of potential secondary schools and key areas can be marked on these. For example, the entrance which is used by the Year 7 pupils can be made the starting point and the main rooms shown. As a guide, these will be the main office, the year tutor's room, the lavatories and cloakrooms, the gymnasium, the specialist rooms such as CDT and ART, the library and the dining room. Simulation exercises on routes can be given and pupils can draw these in. Left and right orientation can be shown and it will be hoped that by the time the pupils visit their secondary school they will have some visual interpretation of the layout. A task for wet play and dinner times could be to build the ground floor of the feeder secondary school from construction activities such as Lego. Photographs of the secondary schools would also be useful.

When the first visits have been made the pupils, especially those with learning difficulties, should be asked to describe what rooms and routes they had remembered on the visit; what was the same and what they found different from the work they had undertaken on the maps. The photocopies of the schools can then be used again to see what they remembered.

Travelling to school
Some pupils will walk or cycle to school with friends or older brothers or
sisters. However, with parental choice and out-of-catchment placement
there will be pupils who need to travel by public transport. For most of the
country this will be by bus or sometimes by rail but there might be some
tube travel in London. Rural pupils might catch the school bus and they
might have even done this to get to their primary school. There are, however,
many pupils who have never travelled on public transport by themselves
and even travelling with friends will bring some problems to those with
learning difficulties. If a bus or train pass is issued, the pupil has to be
responsible for remembering this. Pupils have to be given information as to
what to do if they forget or lose their passes.

One secondary-aged pupil, Alistair, whose independence skills were
very limited, went to catch the school bus but found that he had lost his
pass. Not knowing what to do he started walking home. However,
because of his directional problems he began to walk in the opposite
direction and had it not been for another pupil he might have been lost
or worse. The school learnt after the event that Alistair needed a great
deal of help with social skills, being able to approach people and ask
for help and knowing what to do if something out of the ordinary
occurred.

In the primary school there can be some play-acting situations where
pupils act catching a bus and travelling to and from school. Different
parts can be given such as the pupil who loses his or her pass, who has no
money or who forgets which is the correct bus-stop. Pupils need to know
where the correct bus-stops are and how to recognise their particular bus,
by number or name. They need help with handling money if this is needed
and this can be given in numeracy lessons. It is not possible for pupils to
be sent on an initiative test by travelling independently on public
transport but parents can be encouraged to go with their child as a practice
but allowing him or her organise the trip and carry out the mechanics
of it.

The timetable
Some secondary schools have weekly timetables whilst others have
fortnightly blocks of work. Lesson lengths are also different with some

19

schools dividing up the day into single lessons of 50 minutes or more whilst others have double periods for most subjects. This can come as a surprise for the primary school pupil although with the advent of *The National Literacy Strategy* and *The National Numeracy Strategy* these pupils are becoming used to a particular block of time. What they are not used to is the movement between lessons, although again in larger primary schools there is more use of setting.

It would be helpful for primary schools to organise a 'secondary school week' when the days are split into hour sessions and at the end of each of these the pupils have to pack up their books and writing equipment in a particular length of time. Although an artificial exercise they would then have to line up to leave the room, go somewhere else in the school and return. Then the process of unpacking would occur again in a particular time limit. Teachers in the secondary school are going to expect little fuss and little time taken at the beginnings and ends of lessons for such activities to occur. The primary school teachers will be able to observe which pupils find this particularly difficult and give them extra tips and help.

Equipment and books
Although primary schools have different ideas about books and folders for working in, most of the teachers collect these in at the end of use so piles of these are to be found neatly stacked in the primary classroom. The secondary pupil is responsible for his or her own books or folders unless these have been handed in for marking. Again the primary school can start in Year 6 to encourage the pupils to be responsible for their own books etc. Simulation exercises of packing folders, books, text books and other equipment into the types of bags carried by secondary school pupils can be given. Unless the secondary school has a standard bag, pupils follow fashion so these might be backpacks or sports bags or even trendy carrier bags. Most of these are not suitable for flexible and flimsy books so folders and books become dog-eared. This incurs the despair and maybe the wrath of the subject teacher so guidance on packing is necessary. Adding PE kit, DT equipment and even packed lunches or snacks on top of books can add to the difficulties pupils have with finding what they need. It is difficult for Year 7 pupils to know exactly what they need for each lesson, for each day and that is why they play safe by carrying all their belongings with them.

John has specific learning difficulties, with one of his main problems being an extremely poor memory for daily organisation. He carried a very large sports bag containing all his books, his folders, his equipment and his games kit. As the term went on his books and papers became dirty and torn. Unless his mother took out his games kit this was never washed. In consequence John was often in trouble from his teachers. He could have been helped both before transfer and in his secondary school. Hints could also have been given to his parents.

Remembering to bring pens and pencils etc. is sometimes difficult for pupils who have been used to their teachers in the primary schools providing what is missing. Often secondary school teachers are not able to be organised in this respect and they expect their classes to be self-organised.

One primary school helps Year 5 and Year 6 pupils to learn how to organise themselves for lessons requiring writing. Their teachers have produced an aide-memoire which is well printed, easy to read and which can be either fixed to the desk or stuck in each writing book. It states:

Have you got?

- 2 sharp pencils
- a rubber
- a pen
- a ruler
- coloured pencils or felt-tip pens.

These can be adapted for the needs of each school or subject area and for those pupils whose reading is limited, a drawing of the object can be placed alongside the words.

In order to be organised, being able to read their timetables is very important for secondary school pupils.

Timetables

It is not usual for pupils in primary schools to work from timetables and if they do, this is often from a class timetable. In the secondary school they are expected to copy their form timetable accurately and then read it and follow it. A weekly timetable can cause problems and a fortnightly timetable can bring major difficulties. It would be more sensible for the primary school to concentrate on a weekly timetable and let the secondary school cope with one that is fortnightly if that is its norm. There are many issues surrounding timetables which can be taught in the primary school.

These are:

- learning to read and spell (or copy) the days of the week
- learning to read and spell (or copy) the subject names
- understanding that initials indicate the teachers who will be teaching the subjects
- learning to associate these teachers with some kind of mental picture in order to remember their faces
- linking the room names or numbers with the plan of the school
- writing these in pen because many secondary schools do not allow pencil.

Pupils with poor literacy skills will need overlearning and tips for learning to read and spell these requisite words but if they can master these before they transfer, their first tasks within the new school will be so much easier. At least during the final term in the primary school personal timetables can be used and checks can be made with questions such as 'what lesson are we doing on Wednesday after play in the morning?' or 'when will we be doing Art next?'

Tommy was found wandering around the corridors in his large secondary school. He did not know where he should be next. The teacher asked to see his timetable but was unable to help Tommy because she was unable to decipher Tommy's efforts in copying his timetable into his planner. Many minutes were wasted because the only way to help him was going to the main office.

Timetables are also used for homework. Some schools use homework planners or homework diaries and again the primary school pupils can become used to these. There is an added problem with the homework diary which the secondary school staff need to take on board. This is the way homework is so often given as an oral directive in the last few minutes of the lesson. For pupils with writing or spelling problems or with weak auditory memory and auditory processing, this means that they miss much of what they should be undertaking for homework. Even if the homework is written on the board for copying, these pupils do not have time to finish writing it as their copying skills are so weak. It may be difficult for the primary school to teach speed of copying and this is an area which might need to be addressed inside the secondary sector.

> One large primary school introduced homework planners to their Year 6 pupils. All pupils were encouraged to use these by copying down their tasks, making a comment about how they managed their homework, and their parents were also invited to comment. The pupils took these very seriously. Those pupils with particular learning and literacy difficulties were supported by a learning support assistant who helped them with their copying and who discussed their comments etc. on a weekly group basis. By the time these pupils transferred to their secondary schools they were used to this part of the secondary school requirements.

Breaktimes and lunchtimes
In larger primary schools there might be separate playgrounds for Key Stage 1 and Key Stage 2 pupils and there might be different times for dinner or different places for hot meals and packed lunches. In the secondary school there are almost certainly many different arrangements which the new pupils have to learn. The maps of the school should indicate where the canteen and playgrounds are but all other arrangements need to be given when the Year 7 pupil enters the new school. But times of eating can be taught. Most primary schools have a more traditional school day, starting at 9 a.m. and finishing around 3.30 p.m. with the midday break at 12 a.m. Secondary schools often have late lunchtimes, from 1 p.m. onwards, which can make new pupils very hungry. They need to be aware of this. If it is allowed they may need a substantial morning breaktime snack which they should bring from home. Thus parents need to be aware of this as well.

23

Often primary children are concerned about what they can do at lunchtime and it is helpful if the secondary school runs literacy clubs, quiet games sessions or homework clubs which will enable the less energetic or less social to have something concrete to do. Although this will be told to them when they transfer, prior information would enable the primary school staff to discuss options with the pupils.

Many secondary schools run a cafeteria system for food which is different from many primary schools. Year 7 pupils will have to learn how to queue for their food, to cope with food prices and to find places to sit. Working on food prices can be a task for the primary school and can be incorporated in numeracy lessons. Many pupils with learning difficulties find it hard to add money mentally and work out if they can afford certain items. To prevent embarrassment they need simulation exercises which would help them to buy a more balanced diet other than merely chips or beans. The secondary school can provide the primary school with past menus and prices and choices can be made. If real currency can be used this will have more meaning than if plastic coins are given. If pupils have free school meals they will need to know what they can get for the price of these rather than finding that they have chosen something which needs extra payment.

The issue of what to do and what not to do in this 'freer' time is sometimes a problem for the new entrant. School rules will have to be known and understood. It would be helpful if the primary school staff are given a copy of the rules, for in-class, for moving around the school and for the playground, so that they can discuss these with the primary pupils. Comparisons and similarities with their present rules can be made. If the pupils are aware of what they can and what they cannot do when they transfer there is less likelihood that they will inadvertently be reprimanded.

Learning problems
Some of the issues here overlap with the previous section but they will need to be reiterated as one of the major problems experienced by pupils with special educational needs is their inability to cope with the work set. Later there will be discussion about how information about pupils' particular learning problems can be transferred effectively from the primary sector to the secondary sector so that all staff members are able to act on this knowledge. Also there will be consideration about the role of the secondary school staff in helping pupils with learning problems to access the curriculum as efficiently as they are able.

Learning problems in this section are mostly concerned with the skills of recording but there will be mention of reading and listening skills. The one of understanding the range of vocabulary will be discussed first.

The range of new vocabulary
As has previously been mentioned, pupils on transfer to the secondary sector are bombarded by an enormous range of new vocabulary. This can extend from the names given to parts of the building to adjectives used to describe behaviours etc. When pupils transfer they tend not to ask for explanations so many pupils with learning difficulties believe they will never understand what is being said to them. This leads to reinforcing their low self-esteem and expectations. It would be helpful if secondary school staff could go into the primary schools to explain words which are known to cause problems. To help within the primary schools secondary teachers and their primary colleagues could brainstorm possible lists of words which might confuse and then wordsearches or other activities could be devised. Pupils could be encouraged to 'spot the new word' and there could be competitions to see how many new words they could hear and remember. It is very important to encourage pupils to question what they do not understand. Asking for help is something many pupils feel unsure of so modelling and role-play in the primary school can also help with this.

> One secondary school used the phrase '*consistent* good behaviour' and then found out that many Year 7 pupils thought this meant they had to be 'sometimes good and sometimes bad'.

This issue of asking questions is important also when pupils copy from the board or use worksheets. If teachers' handwriting is unclear or if worksheets are photocopied so often that the writing becomes indistinct the pupils might assimilate words that are not actually correct.

> One secondary school found that pupils had copied 'Pinally defeated Pompey'. For all they knew this was another Roman General instead of a poorly reproduced worksheet which was 'Finally defeated Pompey' where the 'F' was so worn it looked like a 'P'. The pupils felt that it did not make sense but they assumed it was a name they did not know.

Recording
The issue of using planners and diaries for recording homework etc. has
been already dealt with. However, even if pupils with learning difficulties
are given enough time for copying down what they have to do there may
still be problems with their handwriting. Many Year 6 pupils still have
large, unformed and immature script and the boxes within the planners are
often too small to fit in all the words. Some pupils have developed a rather
idiosyncratic style of handwriting with curls to letters and open dots on 'i'
and 'j'. The primary school can help these pupils to make their handwriting
conform especially where size is concerned. They can be given specimen
sections where they can copy sentences such as 'answer questions from
page 3', 'plan a story about a lost dog' or 'sketch three items from your
kitchen'. The pupils will not only have to fit the copied work into the box
but will have to write neatly enough so that an adult can read the work.
Often parents will want to help with the set homework but will be unable to
because they cannot decipher their child's handwriting and their child,
because of poor memory problems, will not be able to recall what has been
written.

Jenny was always conscientious and wanted to do her homework. But she
rarely ever managed to copy it all down and when she did it was difficult
for her to read back. Her mother wanted to help but could not read Jenny's
writing. Because Mrs G. did not want to make a fuss and contact the
school Jenny was often reprimanded for her lack of homework completion.

Using the planner effectively
The real difference between pupils with and without learning difficulties is
how they use their planners. It is often assumed that the pupils will see the
usefulness of the planners as a tool for themselves but they often do not.
Pupils need to be able to answer questions such as the following:

- Why is there a timetable in the planner?
- What are their teachers' names in the planner?
- Which teacher takes the class for Geography, Music etc.?
- How can the planner be helpful for knowing what to bring to school
  each day?
- Could the planner be used to help make a weekly (or fortnightly guide)
  which can be stuck to the fridge or bedroom door at home?

An example planner in the primary school can help answer all these questions and be an invaluable learning tool for later secondary life. Often it is pointed out that many pupils with learning difficulties cannot name their subject teachers.

Note-making, note-taking and copying from the board or OHP
Copying is not a very useful exercise especially if the pupil is unable to read all that is written. However, it is an activity which is frequently set in the secondary school classroom. Although it would be more useful for pupils to be given copies of notes to be copied and these to be gone over by the teacher, pupils in the primary school need to be given practice in copying. Pupils with learning difficulties who find it hard to spell will not copy accurately because of being unable to hold the whole word in their visual memories or will be extremely slow as they copy letter by letter. Often they will lose their place especially if the board or OHP is densely packed with small writing. Because of reading problems pupils may also miscopy the adult writing because they are unaware of what the words should be. Copying then becomes a mechanical and rather meaningless exercise. Teachers in primary schools should not labour copying but pupils need to be aware of what they might have to do so that this exercise does not come as too much of a shock.

Ideas for helping with note-taking and note-making are dealt with in the author's co-written book *'Learning to Learn: Developing study skills with children who have special educational needs'* (NASEN). For pupils with learning difficulties who have poor listening skills, weak spelling and poor handwriting working on their own notes can be very difficult. However, simple tips can be given, again so the pupil will understand what these activities are all about.

Examples of these are:

- encouraging the pupils to ask questions when they feel they need clarification of a point
- providing time with an LSA so that discussion of the subject can occur so that pupils can be given extra consolidation of points and information
- providing handouts with key phrases highlighted so that pupils know which words to listen out for
- helping the pupils to understand linear notes where there are clear headings and numbered subsections

27

- encouraging the pupils to write down key points using single words or drawings/diagrams. These can be set out on a page sectioned in boxes so that information is set out in a structured way
- helping pupils to understand information by providing wall charts either as spider diagrams or as mind mapping
- teaching pupils to cluster information themselves by webbing or mind mapping.

Using the library, CD-ROMs and the Internet
Primary schools often have their own libraries although these may be small and not extensively stocked. However, they are usually catalogued but not always using the same system as the secondary school. Secondary school libraries are usually very large with a plentiful and varied stock of books. In the secondary school pupils are given lessons on how to use the library but often pupils with learning difficulties forget what they are told and cannot find books which are suitable for their purposes. In the primary school these pupils can avoid using the library correctly as their peers and learning support assistants are at hand to help. It is important that pupils with learning difficulties are helped to become independent in library skills.

Although ICT is a subject within the primary school, because pupils may share the computers those pupils with learning difficulties can become the passive partner. Pupils with specific learning difficulties might learn word-processing and other computer skills quite quickly but pupils with more generalised learning difficulties often find it very hard to remember all the sequences. Using CD-ROMs and the Internet to find out information is an important ability. Wherever possible pupils need simple step-by-step instructions which can enable them to open the necessary programs. Instructions which incorporate pictures and diagrams can be most helpful.

Listening skills
Pupils with learning difficulties, especially those with specific learning difficulties, often have extremely weak listening skills because of their poor auditory processing and memory competencies. Those adults who are unaware of these problems may feel that the pupils are lacking in concentration and that they are deliberately not paying attention. Some pupils with specific learning difficulties are visual or kinaesthetic learners rather than being auditory learners and they need visual or tactile prompts.

28

There may be occasions in the secondary school when teachers impart information orally for a considerable length of time which can result in what appears to be lack of concentration from some pupils.

Jason had very weak listening skills. At 11 years old he coped at a six year level. This meant that he found processing more than two instructions at a time extremely difficult. In class he fidgeted when he lost the thread of what was being imparted orally. When the class was told what they had to write. Jason only recalled a part of this. Within a few weeks in the secondary school Jason was often in trouble and had the reputation for paying no attention in lessons. If his subject teachers had been aware of his particular problems Jason's school life would have been much easier.

In the primary school there may be fewer times when pupils just have to listen rather than listen and see or listen and do. There are activities which can be given within the primary school to help pupils remember more or take more from orally presented material. For example, short passages can be listened to and questions asked to see how much has been retained. Also pupils can be taught how to 'look' as if they are listening, how to sit still and how to keep their eyes on the adult who is speaking.

Reading
A common problem for pupils with learning difficulties entering the secondary sector is their inability to read fluently, swiftly and with ease. The primary school, through *The National Literacy Strategy* and using specialised alternative methods, will have been focusing on the improvement of reading. Some pupils may read as well as would be expected given their weak cognitive abilities whereas others will have extremely low levels of reading attainment. Some will understand more than they can actually read whereas others will gain little from their decoding abilities. However, within the secondary schoool they will be expected to read texts which have readability levels of nine years and over which will cause them particular problems. It would be helpful if the secondary school could give the primary school a selection of subject words which might crop up in the first few weeks. These can be taught in the primary sector and if not actually retained by the pupils there will be an awareness of what these are. Not only will the words have been seen previously but they can also be explained if this is required.

Issues of relationship

It is difficult for the primary school to help pupils to cope with working with many teachers who might have different temperaments and who might have their own particular ideas about what should or should not happen in class. However, the primary school can talk to their pupils about adults' ways of teaching and could discuss how the pupils can recognise adults' body language or tone of voice and react accordingly. The higher profile of PSHE should help to address this issue.

If pupils feel worried or anxious especially when they feel that things are not going right they can be given some tips about how to cope. Rob Long in his booklet *Developing self-esteem through positive entrapment for pupils facing emotional and behavioural difficulties* (NASEN) also gives ideas which could be used in this respect.

> One school encourages pupils to adopt 'smiley thoughts' when they feel that things are going against them. The pupils have their own idea of what is enjoyable for them (for example, their pet, a sunny day, a rainbow, a bar of chocolate) and when they feel miserable or anxious they have to think this in order to 'smile inside'.

Primary schools should not make a big production about the problems of transfer but if some issues are dealt with either as a whole class exercise or with smaller groups (especially if these comprise the more vulnerable pupils with learning difficulties) then the new Year 7 entrants in the September term may feel more relaxed and better equipped for secondary school entry.

> One secondary school organised the compilation of letters written and stuck them into a book which detailed the worries and fears as well as the expectations of pupils in the feeder primary schools. These were then given to the Head of Year 7 who went through all the issues raised with pupils on her liaison visits to the primary schools.

How the primary school can inform the secondary school about individual needs

Effective liaison between the schools is the key to successful transfer and therefore it is essential for the pastoral and learning support teams to liaise effectively. It has already been mentioned how members of the secondary school staff visit the feeder primary schools but it is recognised where there are a great many primary schools sending pupils to the one secondary school that it is difficult for staff to organise their time to liaise effectively. When this occurs the only liaison might be through exchange of documents.

It is not often that the primary staff visit the secondary school. It would be helpful where the majority of pupils transfer to the same secondary school that the Year 6 class teachers visit the secondary school so that they have personal knowledge of the school and the teachers. In that way they can share information with the pupils when they have their initial visits.

Written information
Although there will be a great deal of written information sent on to the secondary school for pupils with learning difficulties this sometimes gets to the secondary sector after the pupil has started or it goes to the pastoral or special needs staff and does not get to the subject teachers. Pupils may have a Statement of Special Educational Needs, may have detailed Individual Education Plans and have documents relating to the stages of *The Code of Practice*. Because the first few weeks will be most important for pupils in their subject lessons it is important that subject teachers have some brief data which will inform them about the pupil's particular problems. This should enable them to adopt relevant teaching strategies.

Subject staff need more than a list of pupils with learning difficulties (and, of course, other special educational needs or medical problems). However, they do not want to know every detail about the learning need. One side of A4 which summarises problems, strengths and weaknesses and which gives indications as to how the pupil learns or should be taught is found to be helpful. In the author's book *Spotlight on Special Educational Needs: Specific Learning Difficulties* (NASEN) there is a suggested format for pupils with specific learning difficulties. This could be adapted for pupils with generalised learning problems as well and could be written by the primary school SENCO, the primary school class teacher or any support or advisory teacher who might have close dealings with the pupil.

This information sheet
This could start with a short descriptor paragraph which outlines the pupil's particular problem. This would indicate whether the pupil has specific or general learning difficulties and how these affect his or her learning. It would also indicate if there are any emotional and behavioural difficulties which may need addressing. Because some teachers might judge pupils through their written work this descriptor needs to point out the strengths of the specific learning difficulties (e.g. better comprehension than actual reading, good oral ability, good spatial awareness and practical skills) and the way the pupil learns (e.g. through auditory, visual, kinaesthetic methods or a mixture of these). A recent reading and spelling age could also be given. This short section can also point out the problems the pupil might have (e.g. copying from the board, holding an amount of aurally received information in the working memory) and whether the pupil has low or high self-esteem.

The rest of the sheet can cover four areas of learning. These are 'general', 'reading', 'spelling' and 'written work'. A few short sentences are given to the subject teachers as ideas for their teaching. They would set out statements such as 'not to expect as much homework as others', 'to explain work in simpler terms', 'not to expect reading out loud', 'to help with spelling' and 'to give more time for copying'. In a way this information sheet is a type of individual information plan for the subject teachers so it should be short, easy to read, containing manageable and achievable targets but being pertinent and individual to the pupil in question.

JOHN B.   d.o.b. 16.4.89
Z. HIGH SCHOOL

INFORMATION FOR SUBJECT TEACHERS
John has learning difficulties and can read texts around the 9 years readability level. However, his comprehension is much weaker. His written work communicates rather than containing totally accurate spellings and his handwriting is poor. John will find it difficult to take notes from dictation or copy notes from the board and because of a poor memory, concentration and organisational problems will have difficulties with following instructions. It is possible that he will produce less written work and homework than his peers. He is distractible and his behaviour is often off-task. John has low self-esteem. He is a friendly pupil who enjoys practical subjects.

It would be helpful if you would
GENERALLY
- let him sit where you can help without doing so obtrusively
- not always expect as much classwork or homework as others but set limits to be completed
- try and vary the activities and break up sustained activities into smaller ones (small tasks)
- use appropriate language both when talking and presenting written work
- make work as achievable as possible
- examine your methods of assessment and maybe modify these
- involve parents and keep them informed of progress and problems
- use the blackboard as little as possible
- use consistent approaches for dealing with any inappropriate behaviours.

WHERE READING IS CONCERNED
- don't insist on oral reading if he finds this a problem
- help with unfamiliar subject words
- liaise with the special needs department to help teach unfamiliar words or go through work to be read
- help with his understanding of what he is expected to read
- keep your own handwriting legible to facilitate his reading.

WHERE SPELLING IS CONCERNED
- mark written work on content not spelling
- only correct a few errors
- teach necessary subject words - but don't overload
- liaise with the special needs department to help teach necessary words
- allow him to read back the work if words are unreadable.

WHERE WRITTEN WORK IS CONCERNED
- encourage him to smarten up handwriting but don't expect it to be changed
- don't ask him to write out work again unless he has not taken any care
- either give more time or allow another pupil to make a carbon copy if note-taking is difficult.

Some SENCOs in the secondary school collate such information and write these in a common format for distribution to the subject staff. These act as IEPs for use in lessons. For ease of writing, the SENCOs list all the important hints and strike through those that are not relevant for the child in question. These are not as personal as something written for the particular pupil but they can serve the same purpose.

How the secondary school can use the information

Once pupils with learning difficulties have arrived in the secondary sector the staff who teach them can work on two areas. One is that they use the written information supplied to them and the other is to work on the problems which might present themselves (even if these have been worked on previously in the primary sector). Staff who will be involved are form tutors, other pastoral staff, the SENCO and other special needs support staff (including learning support assistants) and subject teachers.

There will be pupils who might not have had any preparation for transfer in the primary schools and there will be those who have been given a great deal. It is to be hoped that the secondary school knows about these pupils and will arrange the teaching and/or support as is required.

Whole school approaches

For all pupils, not just those with learning difficulties, it would be helpful if there was some consistency in teaching style. Schools have rules, rewards and sanctions which should be followed by all teachers and the way teachers use these school structures will impinge on how they teach. However, this does not always occur and many pupils find it hard to remember that they might have to behave in a certain way for teacher A and in another for teacher B. For pupils with learning difficulties, who find it hard to remember who their teachers are, it is doubly difficult for them to cope with vagaries of teaching methods and styles. One would not want all members of staff to act as clones of each other but certain aspects of class behaviour such as lining up, using a pen, putting up hands when answering could be consistent.

Another whole-school matter is that of homework. Pupils have their homework diaries and schools should plan what is given on which evenings and when work should be handed in. There should be set amounts of work or set times taken for this. If a pupil has a learning problem and is slow when writing or reading, homework might take much longer than for a pupil with no learning problem. If there are homework clubs, either at lunchtimes or after school, supervising members of staff can judge the length of time taken on work. Liaison with the home could give similar results. It would not be of benefit to the pupil if he or she took double the time of the more able peers to produce a piece of work.

35

Because one secondary school felt that the issue of copying down homework was of particular importance it organised a 'buddying' scheme for homework diary entries. Therefore, all vulnerable pupils always have their homework written up for them in their homework diaries and they know this will not be a problem before they even arrive in the secondary school.

Consistency is hoped for where any behavioural issues are concerned. Rob Long has written a helpful booklet which gives information about this area entitled *Supporting Pupils with Emotional and Behavioural Difficulties through Consistency* (NASEN). Although no booklet seems to be in production about consistency of teaching styles, spelling and marking policies, homework issues etc., secondary schools would be well advised to have certain commonalities for staff so that pupils and parents are aware of important points. In this way pupils will have less to remember.

Organisation and learning issues
It is not the intention of this book to revisit issues that have been discussed earlier unless there are very particular points which the secondary sector can work on. Most of the organisation and learning issues already mentioned can be taught in the first weeks of the secondary school and there is the possibility of the special needs department taking a lead in this, before the programme of literacy skills are worked on. Also form tutors can play a role, especially keeping an eye open for those pupils who are obviously having problems.

Secondary school staff should attempt to make the school as easy to access as possible. From the pupil entrance there should be clear directions to teaching blocks and other areas. Maps which are large and uncluttered with 'you are here' arrows can help those pupils whose sense of direction is limited. Many schools have boards with photographs of all the secondary school adults pinned to it, from kitchen staff to the headteacher. However, often these are over-large for those pupils with problems and it might be helpful for these to be subdivided, maybe into year sections, subject teaching sections and non-teaching staff sections.

One secondary school that feels that the first fortnight is a crucial time where new incoming Year 7 pupils either settle or become distressed has set up what is termed a 'buddy' system. The school attaches two Year 11 pupils to each Year 7 tutor group and these pupils escort the younger pupils from class to class and from teaching rooms to playgrounds and dining rooms for the first fortnight.

Schools could use a model such as this and even keep it in place for longer if need be.

Issues with timetabling and homework have been discussed and the secondary school should make sure that those pupils identified with learning problems are coping with these areas during the first weeks. There is always the possibility that there will be other pupils who find the size of the new school stressful but who have not been previously thought of as having any type of settling-in problem. Pastoral and subject staff need to be aware of these pupils and having identified their needs make sure that something is done to alleviate the problem.

It has been stated that prior knowledge of those pupils with learning problems (and other special educational needs) is most important. Secondary staff should be encouraged to read and note the information about such pupils and to organise their teaching situations suitably. This book is not the place to discuss issues of differentiation but in order for all pupils to access the curriculum areas teaching staff should be aware of pupils' learning styles and learning problems. Any curriculum area which is new should be carefully and slowly taught (such as coping with the secondary school library). Some secondary schools have 'link teachers' within the subject departments who have a responsibility for liaison with the special needs/support department. They attend regular meetings and pupils' problems are discussed. The link teachers then take back information to their own departments. Other schools give a short spot to the SENCO at daily staff briefing meetings or at weekly staff meetings so that again information about individual pupils can be given to all who need to know it. One area which is difficult is getting relevant information to supply teachers or other adults who may come into contact with the pupils with learning problems.

Making sure that pupils with learning problems cope at breaks and lunchtimes is important.

One secondary school organises that during the first week of the autumn term Year 7 are the only group in the lunch hall. In this way they are under less pressure. The lunch staff add up the totals of money spent as the pupils move along the queue in order to allay any fears they may have with possessing insufficient money.

Issues of relationships

Pupils who have to leave their close circle of peers and friends might find it hard to cope with new relationships. The secondary school cannot force friendships to develop but steps can be taken to help pupils to become part of the tutor group or teaching group without feeling too isolated and thus unhappy. In the first weeks of a new school term there can be problems where bullying is concerned. Vulnerable Year 7 pupils can be prey to those pupils who might have had similar experiences in previous years. Secondary schools have to be well aware of where bullying might take place and if it is actually happening.

Before transferring to the secondary school Sonny who had a Statement of Special Educational Needs told his LSA 'I'm afraid of going to the secondary school. I am afraid of the children and of detention and other things. I will get bullied, that's what I've been told, like punching and pushing and teachers don't do anything and teachers make up new rules and "what goes on will go on". I want to stay at this school because of the help I will get.' This information was given to the secondary school and staff alerted to Sonny's fears. He was teamed up with an older pupil who helped him during break and lunchtimes and his new LSA became a mentor who checked on how Sonny had coped during the day. This continued until it was felt that Sonny was well able to cope.

The previously mentioned 'buddy' or mentor system could be developed so that the Year 7 pupil who finds it particularly hard to cope has an older pupil to whom he or she can go if problems arise. Sometimes pupils find it easier to talk about difficulties with another pupil rather than going to an adult. Schools with sixth formers often find that these pupils can be excellent supporters for vulnerable younger pupils.

However, other pupils will find learning support assistants to be the adult with whom they feel comfortable. This is especially so if the pupil has a Statement and has been allocated LSA support. Schools could allocate LSAs to support named pupils at tutorial times and during lesson times. This could help in many ways. The LSA could be a named 'supporter' to whom the pupil can turn when there are problems or to help with learning issues. The LSA can assist with the recording of homework and with understanding and completing tasks in lessons. However, there is the need for balance here as no-one wants the pupil to use the LSA as an emotional 'crutch' so if the pupil after half a term is showing no signs of independence then carefully planned objectives on the Individual Education Plan should be put into action. These would target independence.

One-to-one buddy systems can be organised for the first half-term with the pupil with problems being teamed up with someone else within the teaching or tutor group. A different pupil could be used each week, for this is not to make a firm friendship but to stop the pupil having no peer contact. However, when this project stops care must be taken that the pupil is not left companionless. One secondary school built in dealing with criticism and appraisal within its PSHE lessons. Pupils were helped to become aware by discussion and role play that peer support can provide praise which reinforces the positive aspects of work, behaviour and friendships but also that criticism can be positive. This has to be handled sympathetically but it can help alter problem areas. Within these lessons issues of honesty in action and word were also covered. Often these areas have been covered in the primary sector, especially if the school has used Circle Time procedures.

The induction days run by the secondary school before the Year 7 pupils transfer are excellent for helping all pupils. Pupils can meet a number of members of staff which gives them a 'taster' for the larger school. If it can be arranged it would be most helpful for form groups and the form tutor to meet before the start of the school year. This can prevent unsure pupils from feeling they will know nobody when they start the new term. A pre-induction day for pupils with special educational needs with current Year 7 pupils acting as guides can be particularly helpful. It is important to use pupils because more questions will be asked. Less questioning comes to teachers especially when teachers are not known. Some schools meet all Year 6 pupils with their parents. Members of the Senior Staff see every parent in the summer term to talk over problems, uniform, behaviour policy, pastoral system, rules, rewards and sanctions. Although this is general, parents are able to recall information and they can remind their children about relevant issues. If parents are met then the secondary school staff can gain additional information.

Some schools write booklets for incoming pupils. However, often these are too long and not set out to aid readability. It is important that not everything is written. A fuller booklet can go to parents. A pupils' booklet should contain short informative statements with cartoons for reminders and to help the weaker reader.

The most successful secondary schools will have whole school policies for helping pupils build up relationships with members of staff. Staff will want to be seen as approachable and form tutors will become the link between subject teaching staff and the special educational needs staff so that pupil transfer problems can be dealt with promptly and effectively. Schools need to help pupils to feel they are not alone. Often pupils who find transfer difficult feel that everyone else has been able to settle with ease. The secondary schools have to help such pupils in realising that this is not so.

Adult expectations
Secondary school staff sometimes have expectations of the pupil based on reported ability. Here there might be the problems of under-expectations, especially if the primary school written information sheet has stated that the particular pupil has weak general abilities. There has to be a balance between the members of staff understanding what the learning problems might be and what they might reasonably expect from classwork and homework. Too much 'watering down' of work might lead the pupil to become bored and over-expectation might make the pupil reject the work as being too difficult.

However, there might be over-expectations which have their foundations on family members. If the Year 7 pupil has had older siblings then the staff members might start some comparison based on experience and knowledge of this older pupil. Nothing is worse for a younger child than to be compared with others in the family. Remarks such as '------ was really interested in History when he was here' and '----- always wrote neatly' can harm family relationships and make the younger sibling feel inadequate and that he or she is not being judged in his or her own right. Similarly, difficulties may occur where the older sibling had difficulties, for example, those that could be labelled as EBD. The assumption could be made that the younger sibling will behave in a particular or similar way to the older brother or sister. Comparisons can occur not just where schoolwork is concerned but in the realms of sport, behaviour and personality.

Parents also have expectations about their child's ability to cope. Some are sure that their child will find secondary school life extremely difficult whilst others will find it hard to be sympathetic when their child comes home with tales of unhappiness. Parents might also compare their child with a learning difficulty or an emotional/behavioural problem with an older sibling with no problems. Or they might think back to their own schooldays and attain comparisons from these.

The role of parents, carers and other close family members

Parents (usage encompasses carers and close family members) will be better able to support their child if they understand what is expected within the secondary sector. This should be given orally at parent meetings and by supplying leaflets or booklets which parents can read in the home. However, there can be problems with these methods especially where pupils with learning difficulties are concerned.

Initial contacts

Not all parents attend preliminary intake meetings. Meetings are not always arranged at times which are convenient especially for working parents or lone parents who have other children to care for. Written communication which is sent to the home may not be read nor understood. Secondary schools should be required to work around these difficulties. Some secondary schools which have identified those pupils who might have difficulties on transfer make sure that all the parents are met during the summer term when the pupil is still in the primary school. Although this takes a great deal of time, effort and organisation it is felt to bring benefits in that the parent has had the opportunity to give his or her points of view. Any booklet concerning procedures and practices can be gone through carefully. Ideas about how the parent can help can be outlined. Even if the parent might not be able to support the school as much as would be expected at least all parents have been given the opportunity.

Parents often miss the day-to-day support which can be received in the primary sector once their child has transferred into the secondary sector. Their needs are often not so much neglected as sidelined in the latter stage of education.

Those secondary schools which organise extra special educational needs contacts find that the school-parent partnership is strengthened with the parents realising that the larger school will take on board the learning problems that their children experience. Parents who meet the secondary SENCO and, therefore, who have a face to a name feel easier about their child's transfer.

One secondary school sets up the following for parents of primary-aged pupils to make contact with the SENCO and the Learning Support faculty:

- by telephoning the SENCO directly for an appointment to discuss their child's needs
- by contact with the headteacher who then refers them to the SENCO
- by visiting the school's annual Open Days in the June of Year 5 and on these days the parents can join lessons in subjects of their choice for a morning
- by attending the school's Open Evening for parents and pupils in the September of Year 6.

One small market town in the centre of England has set up a Family-School-Community Link Project. This partnership of schools consists of the comprehensive community school and its nine feeder primary schools. It has four aims:

- pupil support and learning
- training
- support for teachers and parents
- successful inter-agency practice.

A link worker whose background is within teaching offers support to families on request. The information leaflet points out that one such difficult time is when pupils make the transition from Year 6 to Year 7 and that there may be parents who have worries and questions which have not been voiced.

Some schools produce home-school contracts. These are often set up for behavioural issues but more schools are issuing these for areas such as homework, uniform and equipment. If there is a later problem then these contracts can form the basis for discussion and action.

Parents often feel as uneasy as the children when transfer day arrives. The more that can be established when the pupils are still in the primary school the easier the first weeks in the new term will be. If the parents know and understand what their children will be experiencing the more they will be able to empathise and support. Of course, it has to be recognised that many pupils are from parents who have separated, divorced, remarried or who live with another partner. The secondary school should, wherever possible and advisable, make sure that both parents are given the same information so that they can support in similar ways. Nothing is worse for a child than if his or her parents have different expectations and treat the child's fears and anxieties differently.

Practical support
Parents need particular knowledge of the following issues. One is that of homework. They need to know what is expected and this is concerned with the homework timetable and the amount that is expected. It would be helpful for parents to know how much they are 'allowed' to help their child and if they should indicate this in the homework diary. Parents bear the brunt of their child's unhappiness if homework is too difficult or if it appears to take too long. Therefore, they need to know the route to take if it is felt that too much has been given or if they feel that their child cannot understand what to do. There needs to be a clear mechanism which can be taken so that the problem does not escalate.

Another issue is that of equipment and belongings. Most children do not want to be different from their peers and conformity seems to be very necessary for them to become 'one of the crowd'. Therefore, the type of bag which holds the belongings, the pencil case, the pens and pencils, the sports gear and any additional items have to be acceptable in the eyes of peers. This can be difficult for parents, especially those whose income is low. It would be easier if the secondary schools stipulated a type of 'uniform' for sports bags, backpacks and other items of equipment. It would also be easier for the pupil with learning difficulties if there were limits stated for the amount of pens, pencils etc. A pencil case containing two pens and pencils, a rubber and a pack of small 'Stickies' plus a ruler and a note-pad could form the basic set of equipment. Maybe a set of coloured felt-tip pens could be an optional extra. If the pencil case were made of clear plastic then the items could be seen easily and parents could check (without their child knowing).

One secondary school advises the following:

- provide a bag that has several pockets on the side. At least one pocket needs to be big enough for the homework diary and any letters home
- colour code the diary and the pocket
- another pocket needs to be big enough for pencil cases
- provide two pencil cases. One is for basic equipment and the other for extras plus some replacement basic equipment
- these cases should be of clear plastic cases so contents can be seen easily
- provide lots of replacement supplies ready at home
- label everything.

It is also sensible for parents to organise phone numbers of pupils who are friends of their child so these can be phoned for information should this be necessary.

A spare timetable needs to be given to the home so that the parents can check on when other items of equipment such as games or swimming kit or particular items for subjects such as CDT need to be taken. It is not suggested that parents should organise these but they need to be aware when to prompt their children. If pupils have everything they need on each particular day of the week they will not be given the extra worry about what might happen if they forget something.

Emotional support
This is a difficult area as parents can be pulled between school and their child if the latter appears unhappy and anxious about school. This often manifests itself in their child giving illness (such as severe headaches or tummy aches) as an excuse not to go to school on a particular day. Or he or she may return home from school morose and uncommunicative, sometimes even crying when asked about school. The child may be negative about school experiences and cannot seem to say anything positive about lessons, free time or peers. When one or some of these behaviours occur some parents feel that this could be a normal part of the process of transferring schools and that 'they will grow out of it'. Others rush in to support their child against the school without finding out the root problem. Some collude with their child and allow them to remain at home. As stated, knowing how to act is difficult for parents.

They need to be aware of the best way to cope with problems such as these. There needs to be a clear route organised within the school for parents to voice concerns. Pastoral staff or special needs staff should be alerted to pupils' emotional behaviours in the home as quickly as possible so that systems can be put into place to overcome these. It is possible that the pupil shows no signs of anxiety within school but school staff have to take the parents' statements seriously. Some pupils are able to seemingly cope in school but take out their problems within the home.

Parents will support their child emotionally but it is not within their child's best interests if they are absent from school. Other books have been written to deal with school-refusers such as David Philbrick and Kath Tansey's *School Refusal: Children who are Anxious and Reluctant to Attend School* (NASEN) which can be most useful for schools. However, parents need support with coping with children who have anxieties about going to school.

Conclusion

Pupils remain in the secondary sector for at least five years. Their first few days can set the scene for either good and positive experiences or those that are negative, causing worries and concerns.

Schools should no longer expect all pupils to cope with ease. Not all pupils have older siblings or friends who can smooth their first weeks. Those pupils with special educational needs of varying types often require extra support and help. If this is put into place early on in the primary school and carried on sympathetically into the secondary school then the pupils will enjoy their later school lives and problems will not occur.

As Tom said, 'Before I came to this school I was scared. But it's great. Mrs C. (his form tutor) is brilliant. She always helps me. Mr D. (his primary school class teacher) told me about this school and what to expect. He was right. I like it here.'

References

Long, R. (1999) *Developing self-esteem through positive entrapment for pupils facing emotional and behavioural difficulties*. NASEN: Tamworth.

Long, R. (2000) *Supporting Pupils with Emotional and Behavioural Difficulties through Consistency*. NASEN: Tamworth.

Malone, G. and Smith, D. (1996) *Learning to Learn: Developing study skills with children who have special educational needs*. NASEN: Tamworth.

Philbrick, D. and Tansey, K. (2000) *School Refusal: Children who are Anxious and Reluctant to Attend School*. NASEN: Tamworth.

Smith, D. (1996) *Spotlight on Special Educational Needs: Specific Learning Difficulties*. NASEN: Tamworth.